Ayibobo

Beginning Vodou

by

Manbo Paula Wédo

Rara Cayes-Jacmel

Ayibobo

Cover: Gédé Pé, New Zealand – "Kwa Sen Bo!"

Cover Photo- Manbo Paula Wédo

Cover Design: Jac D Hawkins

Spirit of the Wind – Artist: Kimata '02

5th rd Edition August 2017

ISBN : - 978-1-312-82651-9

Honour & Respect to You, Your

Families & Your Ancestors

Introduction

This booklet, like a drop of water in the ocean, is but a tiny segment in comparison with Haitian Vodou.

Vodou is vast, wondrous and totally diverse.

The Lwa are glorious Beings whose capacities to love and care for us are enormous. The Lwa walk with us and through faith and service relationships of great Force (power) develop with them.

It is this desire to know the Lwa that brings us to the Cross-Roads and Papa Legba who opens the Gate for us. Once on the other side we find ourselves standing at the Great Cosmic Mirror.

Here, in a dimension where everything is possible, we sing, dance and converse with Angels.

Ayibobo

Beginning Vodou

At the Cross-Roads everything meets, Immortal, mortal, Invisible, visible, Spirit and physical. Papa Legba opens the Gates for us and we find ourselves in a Cosmic Marketplace. Here at this Marketplace, everything we ever need for anything is available. Manbo Ayizan walks here upon the pwen of the Marketplace and holds great power.

Vodou began at such a Cross-Roads. Haiti was the richest Island in the Caribbean, producing coffee, sugar, cotton and indigo.

The Plantation owners were amongst some of the wealthiest in Europe; the slaves amongst the most destitute people on the planet. After the Revolution, the Europeans forsook Haiti and the Island was isolated from the rest of the world. As the terrified and conquered French abandoned Haiti, they left everything behind them, and the Haitians incorporated many trappings of Catholicism into Vodou. They fused the Catholic Saints with the Lwa and adopted the prayers of the Church.

The Gédé, who are peculiar to Haiti, recognized themselves and donned the raiment of the Masons.

Now there is Catholic pageantry braided with the drums and dance of Africa, all are blended in the wonder that is Haitian Vodou.

Vodou comes from the Fon language of Benin and we use the term Sogbay-Lisa, which translates: God is in everything , everywhere all at once. So everything that exists is an aspect of God, the essence of God is in all things, plants, water, earth, animals, reptiles, humans.

Vodou teaches us that because this Divine Essence is an all things, then we need to treat all things as the expression or representative of Divine Essence.

Be aware of Spirit in all things.

Within the Society Vodou says we must grow and become aware of the Presence of Spirit in every moment of our lives. In every thought, every word, indeed, every single action we take. Spirit is present. Vodou tells us to build our good character and live a life of victory. To build good character we are given a number of Principals. From the Ancestors of Haiti came the Lwa, Principles, laws to live by

So, Vodou was born in West Africa, the West African Vodou revelation descended from God to our Earth in the form of two Serpents, Damballah and Ayida Wédo.

For the West Africans, these Serpents represent the Ancestors; Vodou is an Ancestral system where the Supreme Being is the first Ancestor, the Mother and Father of us all.

Vodou honours and acknowledges the presence of Spirit in everything. Vodou honours the Soul within each human being and reminds and assures us that we are indeed Spirits inside a physical body and that the Spirit world is everywhere. From beginning to end, the Spirits are with us, guiding and advising us. It is our responsibility to learn to listen to and honour these Spirits.

When we die, our Spirits continue on towards God. Ayibobo!

The Lwa are the intermediaries between Gran Met – God – and ourselves. It is to the Lwa that our Vodou Service is directed and we can turn to them for comfort and support. The Lwa touch every part of our lives, influence every decision that we make and affect everything we do.

They protect us from danger, bring joy and happiness, they walk with us on the road to Ginen and they have a great love for us. They teach us the road to Ginen is also the path of righteousness.   Honour and respect for the Lwa are amongst the greatest skills we can develop in Vodou. The Lwa can also bring misfortune and unhappiness if we do not heed what they have to tell us, but we are always free to choose.

Vodou is about freedom; however, if we pay no heed to what we are being instructed to do, then we should not be surprised when we don't get the desired results.

Everything is interconnected after all. In Vodou we understand that nothing is by chance and there are no accidents.
The Universe is one and everything affects everything else, the threads connect us all.

Nature knows this, our Ancestors knew this and Science finally understands this. Nothing is separate, and we all serve as part of the whole; what we do to another we do to ourselves.
It is greatly to our advantage to do good work.

Be truthful do good, be truthful do good, be truthful do good. It is the truthful that the Divinities support.

African Proverb

Ancestors

God reveals Herself through the Spirits of all our Ancestors and our Ancestors, who are our closest link to God, are working for us all the time. Vodou is Service to the Ancestors, those who are remembered and those who are lost in the oceans of time.

With our voices, thousands upon thousands of our Ancestors sing. Your Ancestors look out through your eyes, listen with your ears and walk with your feet. They feel life through your hands and speak from your mouth. Our Ancestors add their wisdom and knowledge to everything that we will ever do and everything that we do during our lifetime adds to their understanding and wisdom. Ancestors come through our families, through marriage and initiation and their number is countless, spiralling ever backwards to the beginnings of time.

To acknowledge our Ancestors brings vitality to our lives. Our Ancestors are always with us, they guide us, offer protection, healing and advice. These Ancestors are irreplaceable, they make us who we are and we carry them forward into the future. Our honour and memory energizes and enriches who they are, indeed, our Ancestors can become Lwa.

There is great benefit for all of us in honouring them. When we honour and respect our Ancestors, we honour and respect ourselves.

Ancestral Pé

A hallway is quite a good place to build an Ancestral Pé as it is a transitional place. Clean everything thoroughly and cover the Pé with a white cloth, best hand-washed and sun-dried if possible.

Place 9 glasses of water upon the Pé. If you can't, then place a large vessel of water at its centre and change this water often.

Upon the Pé place a small dish of earth from near your home, I also have dirt from my Grandmother's grave upon my Pé, she is still my strongest connection to God as I knew and loved her as a living Ancestor.

Beautify your Pé with white flowers and sprinkle it with perfume. Serve offerings of coffee, alcohol, tobacco, perfume, sweets and favourite foods and burn white candles upon it. Adorn your pé with pictures of deceased relatives and family heirlooms and objects that were special to your Ancestors.

To chat with your Ancestors call their names out loud whilst pouring 3 libations of water upon the floor, to welcome them and then light a candle.

When you are finished, let the candle burn out and the following morning dispose of the food at the foot of a tree or bury it. Don't throw your Ancestral food in the garbage, it is bad manners. Have special dishes for your Ancestral offerings; keep them separate from the day-to-day dishes that you use.

Our Ancestors love us, opening the doors to communication with them is all we need to do. They are always and forever with us, guiding and protecting, their strength reaching back forever.

Litany for the Ancestors

"To all those whose names are remembered,
To all those whose names are forgotten, lost in the Oceans
of Time,
To all those whose bones are buried in and upon the Earth.
To all those whose ashes are scattered to the Four Winds,
To all those who have gone before,
To all those yet to come,
To you, from the living."

Mr. Louis Martinie

Upon rising every morning, pour a glass of water and take it outside. Orient the water and pour it onto the ground and recite the Litany for the Ancestors adding the names of all your Ancestors you can name after the first line.

Honour your Ancestors with a meal at least once a year. This is called Mangé-Mo in Haiti. Prepare your Ancestral food quietly and respectfully. NO salt. Set the table with love and joy, make this an act of great beauty, decorate with flowers and candles, offer wine and spirits, put on some beautiful music

.

Serve the meals, leave the room, close the door and let the Ancestors enjoy what you have prepared and sacrificed to them.

Ancestors' Pé – NZ

This is a wonderful way to show our Ancestors that we remember and honour them. November 1st and 2nd are the Days of the Dead and a perfect time to make your meal.

Orient everything that you use, this will bring your offerings to the Cross-Roads, the pwen of Papa Legba and make your sacrifices to your Ancestors.
Should we forget, the Lwa and the Ancestors would cease to exist. Without the Lwa and Ancestors, there are no future generations. This is a vital balance between flesh and spirit.

In Vodou the Lwa and Ancestors are not distant Spirits and they show themselves in our everyday lives.

"Nan kafou a zanset yo ap tan nou"

"At the Cross-Roads your Ancestors await you".

We are dearly loved and the Spirits have a strong desire to meet our needs; we "sevi-Lwa" - serve the Lwa with sacrifice, honour and respect. In return, the Lwa serve us, bringing success and happiness and providing guidance in difficult times, the process is symbiotic and everybody gains.

To sacrifice is to make sacred and there are many things we can offer them.

"Calling the Ancestors, Ancestors whose names we remember. Ancestors, whose names are forgotten, lost in the oceans of Time. Ancestors connected to us by Love and blood.

Ancestors connected to us by past life progression.

Ancestors connected to us by inheritance and initiation.

Your names are known, your names forgotten.

Your names lost to us in the oceans of time. Your names denied. We give you praise from the living."

Ancestor Invocation from D'Moja

Nations

The most well-known Nations or Groups of Lwa are: Rada, Congo, Petwo, the Nago Nation and, of course, the Gédé Family. There are many Nations and thousands of Lwa; many are personal and Ancestral Lwa residing with Haitian families, inherited generation after generation.

The Rada Lwa are Air; Ancient, cool and patient, they know our hearts and make allowances for us as we travel towards mystical Ginen. The Rada Lwa are considered to be older and more venerable than the other Vodou Nations. They represent the Raisin or Root Lwa that originated in Africa and came to the New World.

The Petwo Lwa, also called Kreyol Lwa, were born in Haiti and are Fire. They work hard and quickly but expect all dues to be paid to them just as quickly. Less patient, they can make our lives uncomfortable until we honour our agreements

.

The Congo Lwa are Water and are famous for their pakets. These Mysteries are the Masters of the art of magic and bring us the knowledge and techniques for making wangas and pakets.

The Nago Mysteries hail from the Yoruba people in what is modern day Nigeria. The Nago Mysteries are the Warrior

Nation, the Lwas of Iron and Fire. The Nago Spirits walk with both the Rada and Petwo Nations.

The Lwa have other names: the Mysteries, the Invisibles and are also known as Angels. These Spirits live below the watery surface that divides our worlds. Their home - The Island Beneath the Sea - lies behind a great cosmic mirror.

Haitian Vodou believes the world inside this cosmic mirror is populated by the immortal reflections of us all.

Anonse O zanj nan d'lo
Bak odsou miwa
L a wé L a wé

Angels in the Mirror

"Announce the Angels in the water, underneath the mirror, he will see, she will see."

It is customary to address the Lwa as mirror images, we greet them in mirror terms and we present our gifts and offerings to them with our left hand.

"I give you to eat with the left hand; it is with the left hand because you are of the Invisibles."

The Lwa in turn greet us with their right. Our Services to the Lwa include honouring them on their Sacred Days and giving them offerings of food and alcohol. We give the Lwa gifts, burn them candles and tend their altars.

Offerings.

When making your offerings to the Spirits orient them East, west, north and south with a small bow or curtsey to each Quarter Make a cross in the air with the object and place it upon the pé or vévé. Learn what each Lwa enjoys in the way of food and alcohol and other things the Spirits find agreeable

.

Do avoid mixing the actual offerings for the Lwa up and keep separate dishes and bowls for each individual Lwa. If possible, leave the offerings under a tree to dispose of them in an honourable fashion. DON'T throw them in the trash.

For those who believe it, Vodou is powerful, for those who practice it, Vodou is empowering.

Author Unknown

Cross-Roads

The cross is the most important symbol in Vodou; the Spirit realm cascades vertically down from the heavens and plunges deep into the water. Our physical realm crosses over this horizontally. Where these two realms intersect is the Cross-Roads, a place of great power where all things come together and everything is possible.

This intersection is the pwen (Point of Power) of Papa Legba; it is Papa Legba who allows access to the other side by opening the way for us.

The Cross-Roads bring us to the Cosmic Marketplace, all things come together, all is possible here. A place of great power.

All physical cross-roads are keepers of this great power; leave the remains of all your work at a cross-roads, leave a few coins for Papa Legba there as a payment.

"Nan kafou tout bagay ap tan nou"
"At the Cross-Roads everything awaits you"

Vévé

Practically every Lwa has a vévé; this is a symbolic mirror image drawing and it is like a personal calling card. Vévé can be likened to a signature which is closely linked to each Spirit. When created, they can transport us to other realms.

In Haiti, vévé are traditionally drawn upon the ground with cornmeal. The Haitian artistry of their vévé is astounding; these beautiful pieces of sacred art are danced away by the congregation who are energized by the Lwa.

Vévé can be used in place of statues or pictures; they can be drawn on objects for the Lwa and on food offerings, chalk is good for this.

Activate your vévé by pouring libations of water and rum upon them, say your prayers to the Lwa and put your offerings and gifts on the vévé.

No dark rum or food for Damballah.

Waterways

Libations of water are offered at the entrance of the Peristyle, the Pé, the drums and the Poteau mitan.

At home, pour libations east, west, north, south and then centre. Water is of great importance. The Lwa travel on the water from the Island Beneath the Sea. Following the sound of the drums they enter the Peristyle through the central Poteau mitan.

In Family Vodou the process is much the same with the water being poured in the centre of the room and at the doors of the room that is being used as the bagi (Temple). Do this to your best ability

.

Water is life and is vital for the Lwas and our Ancestors.
The second time I met Ogun, he stressed to me the importance of the water, telling me to pour lots of water for the Spirits to come.

Salutes

As mentioned above in Offerings, always orient everything to the quarters. That is, turn to the East and hold up your offering, then turn to the West and do the same. Repeat again for the North and South. You can make this into a beautiful flowing movement of respect and honour.

We salute the Peristyle and Lwa with the following salute:

Step sideways to the right, and bending the knees slightly,
do a little bob.
Step sideways to the left and bob.
And finally, step sideways to the right and bob again.

Just a small bend of the knees

Now spin in a circle to the left, hold for just a moment and spin
back to the right, hold and spin back to the left.

Your spins are 3 steps around in a circle and a small pause.
Then
Step to the right and bob, to the left then bob and finish on
the right

The spinning process moves us from one realm to another;
to the left we greet the Spirits to the right the Spirits greet us. .

This process takes us to the Cross-Roads. This salute is
performed with joy and reverence and is performed in the
Peristyle and at all Services for the Lwa. Salute and greet the
Spirits before your Pé

The process can be slightly different method in method
depending on how an initiate is graded in a Vodou House as

there are protocols to follow. I learnt this salute at my kanzo and have seen it, or a version of it in many parts of Haiti. Most Nations also have their own salute. Saluting the Spirits is also part of Family Vodou

.

Make your salutes with honour and respect for the Lwas. Good manners are important to the development of your good character and your relationship with them.

Balanse

The Vodou process of Balanse is one of "swinging" the energies of an object, to change them by swirling them around and at times, even crashing them together.

The spinning during the salute helps prepare us for the Lwa and we move closer to the Cross-Roads. This is not a levelling out and finding equilibrium, but a clashing together of energies which produces power, Force and change.

Prayer

Vodou Services and workings begin with these prayers.

"In the name of the Father, the Son and the Holy Ghost

*

Our Father who art in Heaven.

Hallowed be thy Name

Thy Kingdom come, thy will be done on Earth as it is in

Heaven. Give us this day, our daily bread

And forgive us our trespasses, as we forgive them that

trespass against us

And lead us no into temptation, but deliver us from evil

For thine is the Kingdom. The Power and the Glory

For ever and ever.

Amen.

*

Hail Mary full of Grace, the Lord is with thee.

Blessed art thou among women and blessed is the fruit of

thy womb Jesus.

Holy Mary, Mother of God

Pray for us sinners, now and at the hour of our death.

Amen"

***

The purpose of these prayers is to prepare the astral in order to enhance the Service or working. In the Peristyle the Prayer Ginen follows this is a very important part of Orthodox Vodou.

The Payer Ginen is not often used in Family Vodou; indeed they say the prayers they know. Here is a prayer that can be used with good results to begin your Services. It is from Msr. Ati Jean Andrenor Lundy at Temp Chango Chawa in Cayes-Jacmel.

Honour and respect to him.

"Gran Met mwen, ma Mandé oh
Pou desam pwisans la sou mwen
Pou la lin nan eklere dan la té
Pou m'fé tou sa mwen bezwen fé pa pouvwa oh
O nom ou Gran Met."

***

Minocan

The Minocan is a greeting to all the Lwa that are not being named or called in a Service or working. This is a very important part of your Service. It is good manners and the other Lwa do not feel left out.

"Minocan, Minocan eh
Yanvalou tou le Sen
Yanvalou tou le mo
Hounsis yo segwelo

Nou rivé nan húmfor, nou gwo, nou gwo

Rivé nan húmfor, nou gwo, nou gwo.

Minocan Minocan eh

Yanvalou tou le Sen

Yanvalou tou le Mo

Hounsis yo segwelo."

Translates:

"Minocan, Minocan eh. Greet all the saints, greet the Ancestors. The Hounsisbow. When we come to the Hounfor, we are big, we are big. Come to the Hounfor, we are big, we are big. Minocan, Minocan eh. Greet all the Saints. Greet all the Ancestors. The Hounsis bow."

After the Minocan, chante for the Lwa and begin your work.

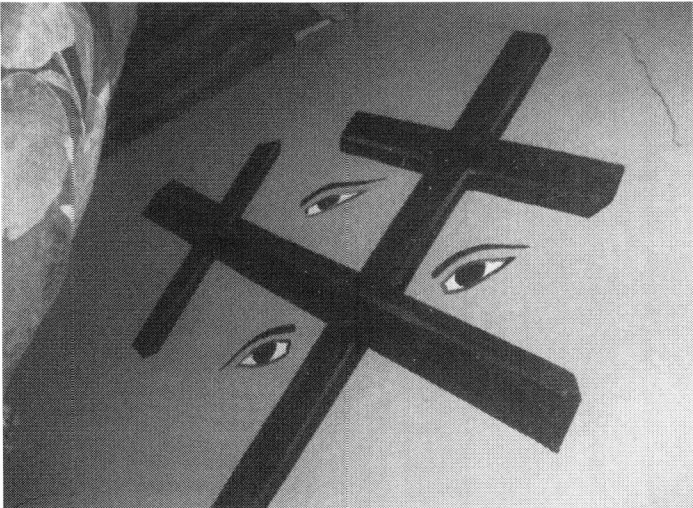

Papa Baz Bagi Auban Haiti

Sevi-Lwa

A Peristyle is a Temple complex where Vodou Services, Actions de Grace and danses are held. Some are large and lavish, others small and personal.

All Manbo and Hougan have their own method of sevi-Lwa and all are different in their approach. The Hounsis sevi-Lwa with singing and dancing, they are the congregation and their energy input is vital to the ceremonies.

These Spiritual societies are centred around the Hounfor or Peristyle and the Manbo or Houngan. Anyone can attend the rituals, Services and prayers and consult the Lwa, Ancestors and the Priesthood.

Music and dance are expressions of faith and joy and play a pivotal role. The Lwa are drawn to the energy as we sing and sweat our prayers.

Vodou Services and sacred objects are crafted to honour the Lwa; these too are used to promote wellbeing, good fortune and all that brings a positive change in life.

Begin to see the world as raw energy that can be shaped and changed as you will it, this is the power of Vodou.

Author Unknown

Vodou is practised by millions in Haiti but only a few are kanzo'd. Family Vodou is everywhere and many of the Orthodox processes of Peristyle Vodou are missing. Family Vodou is personal and intimate and the Lwa come and speak with their children.

One doesn't have to kanzo to sevi-Lwa. if you are bosale and you wish to call the Lwa, use a rattle (kwa-kwa) and a bell and they will come.

The asson is only for those who have kanzo'd and it is considered bad manners by the Spirits if this is ignored. Remember your manners & use a kwa-kwa and bell. Learn what you are able to and work with an open heart. We all as individuals can develop deep and personal relationships with the Lwa.

A libation from your first coffee of the day is always welcomed by the Spirits.

The Angels of Vodou

Papa Legba

Papa Legba is first to be called at any Service or working, regardless of size. Papa Legba is the Guardian of the Cross-Roads and he controls all directions and communications between the Lwa and ourselves. Papa Legba is an old man; he walks with a cane or uses a crutch, these are his symbols as are keys and the cross.

He resides on both sides of the Cross-Roads and is the Guardian of all gates; Papa Legba protects the entrance way of Temples and our homes. We need him to open the way for us, for without him our work is futile.

Papa Legba is the oldest and most powerful of all the Lwa and he decides who can pass, without his consent no human or Spirit may pass through the door way that is the cross-roads to all existence.

Despite this great power, Papa Legba is the Lwa that represents humility in communication. Humility is the way to see virtue or attitude in another person. When we are humble we are open to the views and points of view of others and when we are open, we can communicate with others and a person of grace and power develops.

In Vodou these two things are elevated to the status of Lwa through the auspices of Papa Legba.

"So humble and benevolent is Papa Legba that he never needs sacrifices of bulls or pigs – or even a big party to be made in his honour. He is happy with a modest cup of coffee, a handful of roasted peanuts or grilled corn, even a little tobacco for his corn pipe. Papa Legba moves constantly along the 'big road of life', this is why he is called Met Gran Cheman or the Master of the Great Road. Papa Legba stops here and there, at the entrances of Peristyles and homes alike. There he graciously distributes his advise to all who sevi-lwa."

Msr Max Beauvior – Honour & Respect to him

Become the best Legba you can be, follow the Principle he represents and walk your path with humility and compassion. Lift others up and open the way for them for them to pass. There is much strength to be found upon this pwen Papa Legba is the Sun and The Guardian of Destiny.

St. Peter, St. Anthony and Lazarus are identified as Papa Legba.

"Ati bon Legba ouve barye pou Lwa yo.
N antre ouve barye pou Lwa.
Papa Legba, open the door for us."

Papa Legba's sacred days are Friday and Saturday, his colours are red and white, although some Vodou honour him with purple and yellow.

Offer Papa Legba rum, cigarettes or bones; I give him bones behind the front door. He loves chicken, fried, grilled, stewed, however you want to prepare it. I have also found that he enjoys a pipe packed with tobacco and a big cold beer on a hot summer's day and a hot coffee on cold winter mornings.

Papa Legba's Pé

Make him a Pé behind the front door, add a set of large keys, hang his picture on the wall and serve his offerings there.

When you need him, shake the keys, pour him some rum and call to him. He will protect you and your family

If you are in need of a new home, offer Papa Legba a loaf of bread and some coins, take these to a cross-roads and ask him to find a new home.

Damballah and Ayida Wédo

Damballah and his wife Ayida are the Serpent and the Rainbow and are viewed as the Creators of our modern existence. They intertwine, meet, mix and meander throughout our entire planet. Joined together like the earth and the sky they embody, they are never apart.

They are the Cosmic Parents of all that followed: Damballah and Ayida Wédo are the oldest and wisest of all the Lwa and represent all that is good.

Damballah and Ayida Wédo are the original couple, the Father and Mother of us all and remain the source of all new life. The most benevolent of the Lwa, they are greatly loved.

They make their home in fresh water pools and springs, grace us with their presence in the rainbow and dwell in the thunder and lightning.

Damballah and Ayida Wédo grant riches, bring happiness, good luck and success.

There is a rather beautiful story about Damballah and Ayida: There came a time when they knew they must travel to the New World to their children. They separated one from the other and parted; Damballah plunged into the waters and travelled through the homes of the Ancestors and through places of deep wisdom. Ayida donned the Rainbow as her crown and arched her body high into the heavens, coming back to earth at Haiti. There they joined together once more and brought Vodou to the people.

It is traditional to cover their sacrifices, so that they can feed in private. Cover the offerings with a white cloth and always ensure they have clean water. Always use white when serving Damballah and Ayida Wédo and cover your head.

The Wédo's enjoy flowers, perfume, fruit, white cake, sweet liqueurs, olive oil, eggs and things white and beautiful.

Damballah Wédo

Damballah Wédo

The Great Cosmic Serpent is the Protector of Wisdom and often appears in dreams. He is a most gracious and ancient Lwa who watches over the Ancestral knowledge that is Vodou's very core.

As the manifestation of Da, the force that controls all life; Damballah sustains the world and all that is in it.

Damballah is a comforting Lwa and brings with him hope and contentment. Damballah Wédo resides in trees, springs, marshes and pools.

Damballah Wédo's colour is white, snakes and white eggs are his symbols. Thursday is his sacred day.

Offer him white food; he enjoys a chicken and rice meal served with orgeat syrup.

Damballah speaks through the asson which is also sacred to him

St. Patrick and Moses are identified as Damballah Wédo.

.

Have a white bath on a Thursday to bring all good things from Damballah, use milk, champagne, orgeat syrup, ground almonds and jasmine flowers.

Ayida Wédo

Is the Mistress of the Sky appearing in every rainbow, she manifests in rain storms and lightening. The rainbow and egg are her symbols and she is portrayed as a small green snake. Ayida Wédo oversees fertility, conception and birth.

She is a Lwa who is happy to share and she brings pleasure and joy. Ayida's colours are blue and white, her sacred days are Monday and Thursday.

She eats white food and green bananas. Be sure to cover her food so she can eat in private.

Our Lady of the Immaculate Conception is identified with Ayida Wédo.

The Serpent entwines itself throughout Vodou. One translation of Vodou is: The Snake under whose auspices gather all who serve the Spirits.

In Orthodox Vodou the Manbo and Houngan are the vehicles of these Serpent Powers.

Marassa

In Vodou, twins have great powers, are considered sacred and always become Lwa upon death.

Twins are the physical manifestation of both sides of the mirror and together they represent the human and the Divine, the mortal and immortal. Twins have a connection between the physical and the spirit world, living easily in both.
They have great powers, especially for healing. The Marassa are the Divine Twins and they appear in all the Vodou Nations.

The Marassa's special day is Monday, their colours red and white, and their symbol is a palm frond. They love candy, popcorn, fizzy drinks and toys.

Build a Pé for the Marassa using a toy box and serve them children's party food. Give them their offerings on a red and white checked cloth on the floor.

The month between December 6th and January 6th is the season of the twins. This is a wonderful time to feed them, give them gifts and do nice things for children. Avoid burning candles around the Marassa, they are children after all.

St. Cosmos and St. Damien are identified as the Marassa

Papa Loco and Manbo Ayizan

Two of the oldest Lwa, Papa Loco and Manbo Ayizan are the Ancestral Spirits of the first Manbo and Houngan; they are the Patrons of the Vodou and the Houngan and Manbo of the Lwa.

Papa Loco and Manbo Ayizan are the Lwa of medicine and herbal healing and are often consulted during times of illness. Papa Loco and Manbo Ayizan concern themselves more with those who are kanzo'd.

Papa Loco

Is the Protector of the Hounfor and the Guardian of all Vodou Services. He is very wise, oversees disputes and provides the solutions to any problems with the Lwa

.

Papa Loco is a great medsin fé (herb doctor); he is associated with all plant life and trees are sacred to him.

It is Papa Loco who gives the sacred knowledge of the leaves and plants to the Manbo and Hougan. And it is from him that the Priesthood receive the asson.

Hang your offerings of white rum, bunches of herbs and leaves for Papa Loco in the trees. His colours are white and gold and the red rooster is his symbol.

St. Joseph is identified with Papa Loco

Manbo Ayizan

Manbo Ayizan is the protector of all Manbo and female initiates of Orthodox Vodou; Manbo Ayizan is called during ceremonies of initiation.

With Papa Loco, Manbo Ayizan shares the guardianship of the reverence due to the religious traditions and her healing powers are great. Initiates become the children of Manbo Ayizan and she loves them dearly; she gifts them with great knowledge of herbs and plants for healing and protection.

Manbo Ayizan is often portrayed as an old woman who wears an apron with very deep pockets. She has a good and loving heart and she is the special protector of abused wives and children.

The Royal Palm is her sacred repository and represents her abundance and also the secrets of the Priesthood. When we kanzo we each wear a face covering made from the Chire-Ayizan and this separates us and places us at the Cosmic Cross-roads between the worlds.

Her powers of divination are second to none and she is the patron of the Marketplace where her powers of structure and organization are unsurpassed.

Her colours are white and silver, a shredded palm is her symbol (the Chire-Ayizan), as is the monstrance and her special day is Monday.

St. Clare is identified with Manbo Ayizan.

Ezili Fréda

Beautiful Ezili Fréda exudes luxury she is an adored Lwa who has many children. Ezili Fréda is very feminine, cultured and charming; Ezili Fréda is also very rich and travels around on her yacht (compliments of her husband Admiral Agwé).

A powerful Lwa, Ezili Fréda rules over love and beauty, the home and all our dreams and aspirations. Erzili Fréda grants good health, good fortune and good looks.

Ezili Fréda requires diligence from her children and to be served with respect.

She can't abide the Gédé in any shape or form and gets very upset if they crash her parties. Although some Vodou say that Ezili Fréda and Manman Brijit are grandmother and granddaughter.

Ezili Pé - NZ

When contented, Ezili Fréda gives her children everything they desire. Ezili Fréda loves fine clothing, French perfume, jewellery, lace bordered handkerchiefs, pastries, sweet liqueurs, pink Champagne, French wine, grapes, sweets, flowers, scented candles and mild (white) cigarettes.

Her special days are Tuesday and Thursday and her colours are pink and pale blue.

Virgin Mary and the Mater Dolorosa are identified with Ezili Fréda.

This is the Ezili that we most often hear and read about, but she is so much more. Ezili is the Principal of Love, as humans, of course, we have many ideas and notions about what love is. Vodou explains to us that within the Society love is to know many things and to then be able to harmonize all these differences.

Love creates a channel, a way our differences can be accepted one towards another and then we move forward in truth and in harmony. Without knowledge, love is not possible, Vodou tells us we must develop, and we must build our good character. This is not a sentimental type of love. Love is a powerful weapon built on knowing and respecting others.

Gran Met Ezili is the Great Mother. She is the Mother of all things and incredibly powerful. If it were not for her there would be no harmony.

So you see, Ezili is so much more than the rich fair skinned spoilt woman who paints her nails and cries a lot. This is indeed a far cry from the great Force of love that she truly is. Love – Ezili - is the partner of courage – Ogun – she is the one that brings balance so that courage does not become excessive or reckless.

Ezili comes and puts it all together, puts everything in its place so that everything to grow and develop in harmony.

Papa Ogun Feray

Papa Ogun is Fire and Iron and he greets his children with flaming handshakes. Papa Ogun is fierce and his temper ignites when he comes across injustice. He once told me that he never plays.

This family of Lwa are from the mighty Nago Nation and embodies everything masculine. Papa Ogun rules over everything to do with fire, metal, machines and war.
All those who work with any kind of metal tools or machinery, from surgeons to barbers, from truck drivers to soldiers, all are

in his care. Without Papa Ogun there would be no farms and no food; Papa Ogun is vital for our everyday life.

Papa Ogun is an awesome protector and guards his children with great Force. Within the Vodou Society Papa Ogun is the principle of courage and courage means truth and justice for all. Papa Ogun will speak for us, he has the right to speak because he has courage and he knows that he speaks the truth.

Truth is a very powerful factor in the development of our good character as we travel towards the homes of our Ancestors.

Papa Ogun's special days are Wednesday and Saturday, his colours are red and also red and blue.

His symbols are the machete driven into the earth with a red mushwa wrapped around the hilt and red military uniforms.

Make him a meal of fried beef with red beans and rice; he loves 5 Star Barbancourt Rum and cigars. His energy is very strong and it is good to feed him often. The Ogun Family belong to the Nago Nation.

St. Jacques is identified with Papa Ogun where he is depicted on his white charger.

Admiral Agwé and La Sirene

The Lwa, Admiral Agwé and La Sirene are the royalty of all the seas and oceans. This is their dominion and they rule over everything in it and everything that travels upon the water and they are very rich.

Papa Agwé

Likes to be known as Admiral Agwé and is the Patron of all sailors and fishermen. Admiral Agwé is handsome, fair skinned with green eyes and dresses in the uniform of a Naval Officer.

He enjoys all things nautical from the sound of gunfire to flag signalling and small rafts of food are set afloat in his honour during his Services.

His symbols are miniature boats, oars and metal fishes.
His special day is Thursday.

Most Services to Admiral Agwé are held on the ocean or at least the shoreline. Admiral Agwé enjoys French champagne, liqueurs, cake and fine cigars; his colours are white and blue.

St. Ulrich is identified with Papa Agwé

Barque for Admiral Agwé – NZ

La Sirene

With milky white skin, long flowing blond hair and a fish tail, La Sirene is a femme fatale. She is all at once everything that is beautiful and terrifying in the ocean.

The Patron of Musicians, La Sirene creates her watery music which floats up to the surface from the ocean floor. When La Sirene speaks her voice is sing-song and dreamy and her eyes are wide.

Her special day is Thursday and her colours are blue and green. She enjoys champagne and sweet wines, perfumes and combs.

Her symbols are mirrors and seashells.

Our Lady Star of the Sea and St. Martha are identified with La Sirene.

La Sirene Pé

La Baline

The whale is her Petwo side; she is black and frequents the deep. Powerful and at times menacing, all the mysteries of the ocean are known to her.

***

Go to the sea with 7 silver coins and a large jar of molasses; wear clothing you are happy to throw away. Walk out into the water and fling the coins as far as you can, then turning in a circle to the right, asking for all the things you want, pour the molasses around you. Walk out of the water, change into fresh clothing and throw the old wet clothing away.

***

Make a Pé at the water's edge for La Sirene; give her flowers and pastries and pretty little cakes with blue and green icing.

Never offer La Sirene seafood as a sacrifice.

Simbi

Simbi is the Master Magician and oversees the making of all Vodou charms. A Fresh Water Lwa, Simbi is guardian of all, from ponds and springs to streams and raging rivers. The rain too is under his authority, as is the power that surges through power cables and phone lines.

Simbi is shy. Leave his offerings beside a stream or spring and when he is ready he will make himself known to you. Simbi is often depicted as a green snake.

His special days are Tuesday, Thursday and Friday; his colours are white and green.   Serve him eggs or a mango, cut this up and place in a calabash.

The Magi and Moses are identified with Simbi

The Gédé

The Gédé are completely Haitian in origin.   They are a large family of Spirits who oversee everything to do with death and are knowledgeable on just about everything.

They have access to, and are the keepers of all our Ancestral wisdom.   Their healing powers are enormous and they adore children and protect them with their own peculiar passion, the Gédé are a force to be reckoned with

.

The Gédé are well known for their undignified approach to the living and have a powerful sexual presence whenever they arrive.

The Gédé's special day is Saturday, their colours are purple and black, skulls, black crosses and shovels are their symbols and they enjoy peppered rum, cigars and black coffee.

St. Gerard is identified with The Gédé.

Baron Samedi

Controlling the passage between the worlds of the living and the dead is Baron Samedi. He is the most powerful of the Gédé, and one to be treated with the utmost respect. Without his permission, no soul may pass into the Ancestral homeland and no spirit may return to the Visible world to become an Ancestral spirit, or an Immortal Lwa.

He rules over the Gédé with his wife Brijit.

His special day is also Saturday and he enjoys coffee, rum, cigars and cigarettes.

Manman Brijit

The wife of Baron Samedi and one of only a few female Gédé, Manman Brijit is a powerful and terrifying Lwa, especially if she is not honoured properly. She can destroy everything we have strived to achieve if she determines it to be disrespectful. Manman Brijit can also be our most powerful ally; she is a wise and powerful judge.

Manman Brijit is the Guardian of the Cemeteries and the Queen of all Ancestors. A white skinned Lwa, she is a fearless tough woman who curses a lot and always wears purple.

Her special day is Sunday and she enjoys black coffee, chocolate and cigarettes.

St. Brigid is identified with Manman Brijit.

The first man and first woman buried in any cemetery become Baron Samedi and Manman Brijit. Leave your offerings for them on these graves and tend them with vigilance
.

The Baroness is always honoured at the gate of the cemetery, while the Baron is honoured on the way to the cemetery.

Days of the Dead Parade. Jacmel Haiti.

The Days of the Dead, November 1st and 2nd, are a perfect time to honour the Baron, Manman Brijit and the Gédé; it is also a time of reverence and care of the Ancestors.

At this time, Haiti explodes with the Banda. The Gédé, in sunglasses and dressed in purple and black, wander about. The energy is electric and people dance and go crazy in the streets.

Festive Days of the Lwa

In Haiti the Lwa are honoured at certain times of the year with pilgrimages and Festivals. These are sacred to the Lwa and have great Force behind them.

6th Jan:	Mangé Marassa -
7th Jan:	Simbi d'lo.
20th Jan:	Gran Bwa
1st Feb:	Manman Brijit
2nd Feb:	Oya Yansa
22nd Feb:	St. Lucy
25th Feb:	Mangé tet d'lo. - Feeding of the springs
17th Mar:	Damballah Wédo (St. Patrick's Day)
17th Mar:	Rara begins
19th Mar:	Papa Loco (St. Joseph)

19th Apr:	St. Expedite
23rd Apr:	Legba Petwo (St. George)
25th Apr:	Criminel (St. Mark)
15th May:	St. Dymphna
13th Jun:	Legba (St. Anthony de Padua)
24th Jun:	Ti Jean Baptiste-Petwo
28th Jun:	Ezili
29th Jun:	Legba (St. Peter)
16th Jul:	Damballah Wédo
16th Jul:	Ezili.
16th Jul:	Pilgrimage to Saut d'Eau
22nd Jul:	Mary Magdalene
26th Jul:	Ezili Fréda and St. Anne
29th Jul:	La Sirene (St. Martha)
11th Aug:	Manbo Ayizan and St. Philomena
15th Aug:	Assumption Day This is a very important day in Vodou.
31st Aug:	Admiral Agwé
27th Sep:	Marassa
28th Sep:	St. Michael
2nd Oct:	Oya Yansa
16th Oct:	Gédé (St. Gerard)
1st and 2nd Nov:	Days of the Dead
11th Nov:	St. Martin de Cabellero
22nd Nov:	St. Cecilia
25th Nov:	Mangé Yam. Harvest Festival in "Ayiti.
4th Dec:	Chango

12th Dec: Virgin of Guadalupe

13th Dec: St. Lucy

17th Dec: Legba (St. Lazarus)

25th Dec: Baths and bonfires to invigorate the Lwa.

31st Dec: In Haiti, the Manbo and Hogan do Spiritual work for the upcoming year.

Dancing with the Spirits. Rara Cayes-Jacmel

There are so many ways to sevi-Lwa on any of these Annual Festival days offer special food and give them gifts. Dress in their colours, do some good work or charitable act of kindness in their name.

Remember this is all about the development of your good character as you walk towards the homes of your Ancestors

Hold Services in their honour and sing and praise them. These are also good times to forge strong links and make requests of the Lwa by taking sacred baths and performing Actions de Grace.

Chante Vodou

In Haiti, the rhythms of the drums are usually fast paced and the chants and the drumming are quite different to each other.

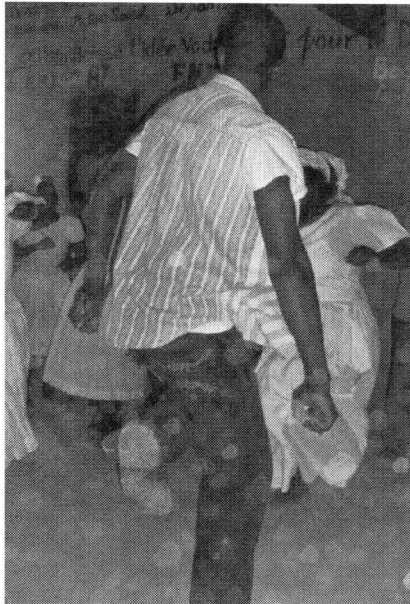

Temp Chango Chawa. Cayes- Jacmel

At Services the chants are all call-and-answer with the Manbo, Houngan and congregation offering a joyful noise unto God.

Take your time and once you know the words bring your chante up to speed. Never be afraid to invent your own songs, the Lwa will love it.

La Fanmi Assemblé

La fanmi assemblé, la fanmi assemblé a-e-oh
La fanmi assemblé, la fanmi assemblé nou.

*

We will greet the Lwa, we will greet them a-e-oh   x2

*

La fanmi assemblé......... (chorus)

We greet Lwa......Legba, Loco, Ayizan, Marassa, Damballah Wédo, Ayida Wédo, Papa Agwé, Miss Ezili, Papa Ogun, Gédé.

We greet each Lwa in turn and sing the chorus in between each Lwa. More Lwa can be added to this chant, if that is the case, Rada first, Petwo second and the Family Gédé at the end.

Manbo Paula

***

Papa Legba

Verse One.
Legba nan baye- a. Legba nan baye-a Legba nan baye – a. Si ou ki poté drapo.

Si ou k ap pare soley pou Lwa yo.

Verse Two

Legba dans h'umfor. . Legba nan baye-a Legba nan baye – a. Si
ou ki poté. Drapo. Si ou k ap pare soley pou Lwa yo.

***

Nou marché Papa Legba nou marché

Nou marché vyé kia an, nou marché

Nou pralez wé saki nan kai-la

Nou pralez wé koté Legba komandé.

***

Papa Legba open the door wide, Papa Legba, here are your
children. Papa Legba open the door wide,take us safely to the
other side.

Odu Legba....Papa Legba
Open the door.

Louis Martinee

Bonju Papa Legba, bonju ti moun wé oh.

M'apé mondé o komoun on yé

Bonju Papa Legba, bonju ti moun wé oh (x3)

Legba ai-o, Legba ai-o, Legba ai-o

Papa sé oh ley

Ai enema Legba Papa soley (x3)

*

Komandé o, komandé o

Papa Legba komandé

Vodou Legba komandé

Kommandé o (x3)

Papa Legba komandé , vyé Legba komandé

Vodou Legba komandé

Komandé-o komandé-o.

D'Moja

Ancestors

Yay yay bon gay. Yay yay bon gay.

Ah-ah-ah.   Yay yay bon gay.

***

Wohl-wa Egungun.   Wohl-wa Egungun.

Wohl-wa Egungun.   Wahl-wa.

***

La Sirene

La Sirene, La Balin, chapo m'tombé na la mer

La Sirene, La Balin, chapo m'tombé na la mer

Map fe karese pou La Sirene, chapo m'tombé na la mer

Map fe karese pou La Balin, chapo m'tombe na la mer

Ooooohhhhh.

***

Simbi D'lo

Simbi D'lo, Yehwe, Damballah Wédo Yehwe

Simbi D'lo Yehwe, Damballah Wédo Yehwe

Simbi yo poko konnen mwen,

Simbi yo poko konnen mwen-la
Simbi D'lo, Yehwe o.

***

Gran Bwa

Gran Bwa, zile, zile-o
Gran Bwa mote bwa L'ale ...Aaa die
M'ale la Gran Bwa
M'pralé keyi fey mwen.

***

Ezili

Ezili fré li fré li Fréda, Ezili fré li fré li Fréda
Ezili o yon pa mangé moun anko
Inosan Bondyé va gadé yo
Ezili fré li fré li, li yo bel fam
Ezili fré li fré li yo fam blanc
Ezili o yon pa mangé moun anko
Inosan Bondyé va gadé oh.

***

Mahi Pou Ezili Fréda

Ce chance oh! O, ce chance o
Ce pas wanga ou gangnin. Ce chance oh!
Grande Ezili Fréda Ce chance ou gangnin

Ce pas wanga ou gangnin
Ce chance O Matresse.

***

Ezili nana o, Ezili nana o, Ezili nana o ya ga sa
La rosé pap rete tu tan, soley pa reveyé
La rosé pap rete tu tan soley pa reveyé
Ezili nana o, Ezili nana o, Ezili nana o ya ga sa.

***

A nou bel fam, Se Ezili?
Ezili m'a a fe nou kado. Ava ou ale.
Ayibobo

***

Papa Loco

Papa Loco nou la ago-é x2
Papa Loco nou la
Papa Loco nou lensifre
Batala 'oungan mwen.

***

Damballah Wédo

Damballah Wédo se bon, se bon
Damballah Wédo se bon se bon
Le ma sele chwal mwen poum fé le tou peyi a
Le ma retounen gen moun kap criyé

Le ma retounen gen moun kap rele.

Papa Baz

***

Damballah Wédo, behold your children hey!
Ayida Wédo, behold your children hey!
Damballah Wédo, behold your children oh
Oh ye-ye oh....We are your children.

In Kreyol

Damballah Wédo, gadé pitites ou yo he!

Ayida Wédo min pitites, ou yo he!
Damballah Wédo gadé pitites ou yo he!
A yé-yé oh
Damballah min z'enfants ou la.

***

Koulev O

Koulev, koulev O
Damballah Wédo, Papa ou koulev O
Koulev koulev O

M'apé rele koulev. Koulev pa palé
Damballah Papa ou koulev O
Si nou wé koulev. Ou wé Ayida Wédo
Si nou koulev. Ou wé Damballah Wédo
Papa ou koulev O.

***

Ogun

Ogun. Oh rere a rere oh- Ogun.

D'Moja

***

A mwen Feray-O
Se pa Jodi a yo lome nom mwen
A mwen Feray-O
Se pa Jodi a yo lome nom mwen
Depi aye yo lome nom mwen

Depi aye yo lome nom mwen
A mwen Feray-O
Auko mwen danjeré.

***

Ogun Fé, Ogun Feray-O
Ogun Fé, Ogun Feray-O
Ou pa wé m' inosan
Ou pa wé m' inosan
Bo Tagi yu vle Touye
Chwal mwen.

***

Ezili Danto

Barak, barak, ooo
M Pa bezwen yon fanm ki jalou trop ooo
Si m'pran yon fanm ki jalou Ezili Danto
Barak kondi m'ale nan simitye.

***

Bosou

Papa Bosou papa m'ap di wou
Bonswa tigout d'lo mape gete
Tral ale ale le la
Retouner l'ap di rou mesi.

***

Zaka Mede

Minis Azaka m'ape diwou bonswa
Bonswa a o miniso Azaka m'ape diwou
Bonswa bonswa ominiso aupwal nan

Paxotiwo move tan bareim.

***

Kouzin Zaka

Bonswa Kouzen bonswa
Kouzen o (x2)
Kan yo we mwen konsa mwen danjere.

Angels in the Mirror

***

Apré Dye

Sé Dye nou pé apré Dye bon Manbo mwen
Sé Dye nou pé
Sé Dye nou pé apré Dye bon Manbo mwen
Sé Dye nou pé
Pasé pa sevi pwen-mwen. Pito mele melo
Apré Dye bon Manbo mwen.

***

Baron

Baron m'ap di ou boswa a
Si pitit ou ki vinn nam pye ou

Ouve rant pau mwen, mwen pa kapab

Amko se pititi ou mwne ye

Se nan pye w paum vini.

***

Manman Brijit

Manman Brijit Manman mwen!

O! Ou oue ca

A'entour caille-la

Gangin dif e la-dans ni

Nous chace bois

Pou nou sememble di fe

Nou chache d'lo pou nou

Touve dif é

La plus pa tombé

Ou pas oue

Terre-La glisse?

***

Gédé

Gédé with your top hat. Gédé it does not fall

Gédé with eyes in both worlds...

Gédé Gédé Gédé.

He's drinking rum with strangers

Gédé drinks rum with strangers.

Kerry Simpson

Favé Étonan

Agwé, Ezili Gran son sa a dous

Ki sové yon mizé tankoum

Yon fwa mwen té pedi

Mae kounie-a yo jwen mwen

Mwen té aveg man kounie-a a mwen wé

Favé étonan.

Amazing Grace

There are thousands of songs for the Lwa, many of which can be found on the internet.

Le Grand Recueil Sacre. Ou Repertoire des Chansons du Vodou Haitian.

This is a book that I would recommend is by Bon Hougan Msr. Max Beauvoir - honour and respect to him. He has collected over 1,700 songs and chants.

A Method for Calling the Lwa

"In Vodou we use all the elements in Nature. Water-Air-Fire and Heart, plus the vibration of Nature with the drums. And you just let go"

Conversation Msr Boutin

Here is a simple method that you can use to call the Lwa. It contains small pieces of the Prayer Ginen and is a process you can use for Services you wish to perform for the Lwa.

It is a mixture of Creole English and French and has been used many times in our Services with good results.

Prepare as much as possible before the Service. This the time to build the Pé, make sure that you have all the offerings ready and draw any vévé you are using.

In Haiti, they lean forward from the waist with one leg slightly in front of the other and taking small amounts of cornmeal roll it through their finger tips and draw the vévé.

Begin your Service by clapping your hands 9 times in 3 groups of 3 (clap, clap, clap, and pause, repeat until you have clapped 9 times). Now, clap your hands 9 times quickly, do this 3 times and finally repeat the first handclaps. So it goes 3,3,3, 9,9,9, 3,3,3.

Now it is time to rele Lwa yo (call out to the Lwa). You can also use your kwa-kwa and bell to call each Lwa as you proceed through your Service.

Saluting the Peristyle Auban Haiti.

Rele

"In the name of the Father, the Son and the Holy Ghost

*

Our Father who art in heaven,

Hallowed be thy Name

Thy Kingdom come, thy will be done on Earth as it is in

Heaven

Give us this day, our daily bread

And forgive us our trespasses, as we forgive them that

trespass against us

And lead us no into temptation, but deliver us from evil

For thine is the Kingdom

The Power and the Glory

For ever and ever.

Amen.

*

Hail Mary full of Grace, the Lord is with thee

Blessed art thou among women and blessed is the fruit of

thy womb Jesus.

Holy Mary, Mother of God

Pray for us sinners, now and at the hour of our death.

Amen

*

A l'Esprite soutout royaume de Bondye

*

Gran Met mwen, ma Mandé oh

Pou desam pwisans la sou mwen

Pou la lin nan eklere dan la té

Pou m'fé tou sa mwen bezwen fé pa pouvwa oh

O nom ou Gran Met.

*

Rele tou Lwa yo dan la syel. Rele tou Lwa yo nam la té.

*

Minocan, Minocan eh

Yanvalou tou le Sen

Yanvalou tou le mo

Hounsis yo segwelo

Nou rivé nan húmfor, nou gwo, nou gwo

Rivé nan húmfor, nou gwo, nou gwo.

Minocan Minocan eh

Yanvalou tou le Sen

Yanvalou tou le Mo

Hounsis yo segwelo

***

Chante   La Fanmi Assemble

Salute your Peristyle or Bagi

Take water that you have already consecrated and begin by pouring 3x libations at the entrance or in the east and salute.

Pour 3x libations of water at your pé or in the west. (This does not imply that your pé has to be situated in the west, this is just the process of the waterways.)

Pour 3x libations to the north and then to the south. Pour 3x libations in front of the drums if you are working with drummers. It is very important to acknowledge the spirit of the drums.

Finally, pour 3x libations in the centre of your Peristyle at the Poteau mitan. It is appropriate for someone to salute these points with a candle at the same time the water is offered.

When you are finished, return the candle to the Pé or the floor and place the water in front of the pé. In Haiti they use a really big enamel mug to carry the water for the libations. They call it the cooling pitcher and during ceremonies it is used often, pouring libations to the Spirits.

Cooler things are carried in the right hand, the cooling pitcher for example and hotter things are carried in the left.

Rele Papa Legba   Sing for Papa Legba

"Legba Nan Baye-A".

After the chante to Legba, draw vévé or cross-roads on the floor, pour libations of water and invoke Papa Legba to open the way for you. Offer Papa Legba rum and tobacco, or a meal. Place the offering on the vévé or the cross-roads.

"Ati bon Legba ouve baryé pou Lwa yo. N antre ouve baryé pou Lwa m

Papa Legba, open the door for us"

Sing for Papa Legba

"Papa Legba Open the Door Wide".

Sing, sing, sing!!!.

Remember you are raising your energy, heating up and the Spirits will join you. Throw out any apprehension or doubt. Sing, sing, sing!!!

*

70

Rele The Marassa

Call the Marassa and play with them, they love toys and lollies, they are very important. Play, play, play, let go and enjoy the moment.

*

Rele Ancestors

Rele tou sen gason nan l'esyel

Rele tou sam songé et tou sam pa songé

Rele tou sen famn yon nan l'esyel

Tou sam songé et tou pa songé

Pou tou sen gason yo nam la té

Pou tou sen fis yo nam la té

Pou tou pecheur yo nam la té

Pou tou mo, yo ki mwen rele

Et tou mo, yo ki mwen pa rele.

*

Take your cooling pitcher and kneel on the floor, pour 3x libations of water in front of you and begin:

"Respect and honour to the Dead and Gédé Family of Haiti.

To our Beloved Ancestors; you who live in our very bones and call to us from the waters; generation upon generation.

Ago le mo ago

Respect to all those who have passed and Honour to all those yet to come.
Ago le mo ago

Respect to the Mysteries, the Invisibles and the Angels who guide all things in the world under God.
Ago ago-si ago-la."

Dip your fingertips in the cooling pitcher and flick 3x libations over your head behind you when you say, "...have passed".

Dip your fingers in the cooling pitcher again and flick 3x libations of water out in front of you as you say, "...to come".

Stand and return the cooling pitcher to the Pé.

Take up your Ancestor offerings; orient and, holding them out in front of you, call your Ancestors.

"To all those whose names are remembered
To all those whose names are forgotten, lost in the Oceans of Time.
To all those whose bones are buried in and upon the Earth

To all those whose ashes are scattered to the Four Winds
To all those who have gone before, to all those yet to come.
To you from the living."

Louie Martinie

Place your offerings upon the Ancestors vévé or Pé and commence your singing to the Ancestors.

*

Chante   "Yay Bong Gay"   and "Wahl Wa   Egungun"

Sing, sing, sing, sing sing!

*

Continue the Service this way, call the Lwa and give your offerings, make your requests, singing and saying your prayers until you have finished work. Remember heat is energy rising, work hard sing and dance. Make all your offerings to the Lwa you are calling, remember to salute them.

*

Orevwa

Finally, thank the Lwa, in the reverse order you called them, saying...

"mesi anpil (name the Lwa) m'ale, m'ale."

This is literally just a very simple thank you and goodbye. I have written down the last of the order you add the Lwa you have called ensuring the last one you called is the first one you say good-bye to.

"Respe hone le mo et la Fanmi Gédé a A'yiti., m'ale m'ale

Mesi anpil les Marassa., m'ale, m'ale.
Mesi anpil Papa Legba., m'ale, m'ale.
Mesi anpil tou Lwa yo dans la syel., m'ale, m'ale;
Mesi anpil tou Lwa yo nam la té., m'ale, m'ale.
Ago ago-si ago-la."

*

In the Name of the Father, the Son and the Holy Spirit.

This process is not a hard and fast rule, add songs and prayers and make your Services your own, trust what you do and have faith, the Lwa will respond to you if they see that you are genuine and respectful in your work. They will teach and guide you. Remember, the Mysteries reveal themselves.

Sing and dance, sing and dance and sing and dance some more, the more effort you put in the better your results will be. Serve the Lwa with love and joy.

I found in Family Vodou that the Manbo or Houngan (Bosale) spoke the prayers that they knew and worked with what they had.

If you are serious and wish to learn the Prayer Guinee, then I would recommend Manbo Chita Tann. She has a CD of the Prayer Guinee. I suggest you join the Prayer and follow her as part of the Congregation. Remember the Prayer Guinee is Orthodox Vodou and not often used in Family Vodou in Haiti.

***

Baths

Baths are best taken on the special day of the Lwa that you are working with, e.g. Damballah's special day is Thursday.

The best-case scenario is that you have clothing or pyjamas to put on afterwards that are the special colour of the Lwa, a head covering to match and sheets that are also colour appropriate. If you have nothing appropriate use white.

Best to abstain from sex for 24 hours afterwards, it is not that sex is wrong or bad, it is just such a potent energy in and of itself , it can have the tendency to neutralize the work that you are undertaking.

Some baths can be taken in conjunction with others but never mix the ingredients of two or more baths together. Vodou is modest, if you are assisting another with a bath be sure that you are both clothed.

Method

Draw the Lwa's vévé on the side of the bath and run the bath. Take all the ingredients for the bath and orient them east, west, north and south. Do this with a bob or curtsey to each direction.

Add the ingredients to the bath be sure to check the recipe, sometimes you put everything in at once and sometimes you don't.

Take your kwa-kwa and rattle it over the top of the bath, do this in circular motion and say the 3 Catholic prayers.

Next, ask Papa Legba to open the Gates, followed by a prayer to the Lwa you are working with. Now, step into the bath.

Always check the procedure of the recipes; some are applied from the feet up, some from the head down. It is a good thing to be as clean as possible when you take these baths, so a shower beforehand is perfect.

Crush the leaves and herbs upon your pulse points, working downwards from your head (unless the recipe says otherwise). Speak aloud that which you desire or that which you are wanting to remove.

When you have finished, pull the plug and step out of the bath, air dry if this is possible and get dressed in the Lwa's colours.

Leave the mixture in the bath, scoop out the following day (use gloves), put it in a bag with some money and dispose of it - not in your trash - cross-roads are an excellent choice.

If you don't have a bath I would recommend you buy one of those large round wash basins. Plastic is cheaper but the Haitians use enamel for their workings. Draw the véve on the side of the basin and follow the same procedure, but step into your shower box and pour or sponge the mixture over you as the recipe directs.

When you are finished, place a lighted candle in the middle of any mixture left in the basin and leave until the morning. Dispose of the mixture the same way as the bath. It is also a good idea to take a purification bath before your work, but do not take them on the same day.

Eg: For a Thursday bath for Damballah, a purification bath would be taken on the Wednesday. Some baths are best taken 3 in a row, you can choose, one after the other or wait a week between each and have it on the appropriate day.

Always do your best to repeat your process as close as possible to your original when doing this.

It is important to pay the water before you take any bath.

***

Saut d'Eau

Although most of the elements of this book are Haitian Vodou, it also has Vodou with my own New Zealnd flavour.

Vodou is in constant evolution, always changing. From the moment people left West Africa to the modern times in which we live. Vodou is like a snake that is in full transformation.

All Hounfour and all Sosyete, are very similar in many ways, but each have their own rules. Those who do not belong to a Sosyete, but practice the traditional Vodou in their space, do with great faith and honour to the Spirits.

Vodou is spirit and everything has a spirit, everything has a soul, everything has a spark of Bondye. Some people need guidance, others practice Vodou in large Sosyete, while others live peacefully in their homes, practicing alone. There are people living in cities practicing Vodou in an urban fashion.

Do your services your way and with what little you have, but remember make the best effort you can. If you have faith and confidence in what you do and have faith in the Lwa, they will respond to you and they will see that you are respectful and humble at heart in your work.

A Houngan or Mambo can help you discover the Lwa of your Head, your saints and guardian angels. If this is not possible, dont despair, through prayer, service and diligence the Mysteries will reveal themselves. Not all of us are born for the Priesthood, but everyone can serve their Lwa well.

Sing and dance, sing and dance and then sing and dance some more. With much effort, the better will be your results.
Sevi Lwa, serve your Lwa and your Ancestors with faith, hope, love and joy, and the transformation will begin.

Vodou has many secrets,Rites of Passage and Inititation Cermonies that can never be written or revealed. Anything discussed in this booklet is public knowledge and can be expereinced by anyone attending a Service or Ceremony.

If you have found this booklet and it touches you, know that this is just the tip of the iceberg, there is so much more to Vodou than you could ever imagine.

The path is yours, develop your good character, follow the Principles the Lwas embody and walk with faith and strength towards the homes of your Ancestors. Ayibobo!

Criminel's Peristyle Jacmel

Ayibobo

Ayibobo is an exclamation of praise and amen in Haitian Vodou and it is with praise and love that I offer this work.

To Damballah, who arrived in my dreams two decades ago and who has surrounded me with goodness and Serpentine comfort ever since.

To Ogun Feray, who on our first meeting greeted me with his flaming arms crossed and said he loved me.

To La Sirene, who rose up out of the water and told me she had waited a long time for me in her eerie sing-song voice.

To the beautiful and elegant Ezili, whose love I felt at first meeting her took my breath away.

To Ezili Danto, who showed me that she listens to all who come to her and just how fiercely she will protect them.

To Criminel, under whose auspices I find myself at this time. Criminel's Force is unlike anything I have known.

Finally to Manman Brijit, who surely and steadily reveals herself in my Vodou.

This work grew from a booklet provided to members of The Hounfor du Marché Sociétié Incorporated. I would like to take a moment to thank and acknowledge all those who ever journeyed to the Cross-Roads with me.

I would also like to acknowledge at this time Mr. Louis Martinee, for the wisdom and the tools he provided for me in his New Orleans Vodou Tarot all those years ago. They proved to be excellent foundations to build upon and created in me the desire to go further, look deeper.

I want to acknowledge Professor Bayinnah Bello whose wisdom is truly great and helped me so much on my path.

Honour and respect to you, your Family and your Ancestors.

With much love, honour and respect to all my wonderful Haitian friends and family who shared their songs and wisdom, and Cupidon for patiently translating all my requests.

There are one or two quotes in Ayibobo that I have had written down for years and now, have no idea who the authors are. I would like to also acknowledge their wisdom at this time.

Finally to Msr. Boutin who has patiently provided me with wisdom, guidance and encouragement along my path. Thank you for your wonderful support.

Ayibobo!

Manbo Yvette Temp Chango-Chawa

Manbo Paula 2013

Manbo Paula, a New Zealand-born artisan currently lives with her family and two cats amongst the beauty and serenity of New Zealand's South Island high country.

Manbo Paula began dreaming Vodou in the '90's and formed her Society, The Hounfor dy Marche in '98. Hounfor du Marche later became New Zealand's first registered Vodou Society.

In 2000, Damballah Wédo appeared in her dreams and she married him in aa Spirit Wedding in 2001.

Continuing on her Vodou journey, Manbo Paula kanzo'd asogwé in Jacmel in 2004.

Her Vodou continues in Haiti where she s Sevi-Lwa at Criminel's Peristyle in Jacmel and at Temp Chango-Chawa in Cayes-Jacmel.

Family Vodou has become of her Vodou. Here contact with the lwas is personal and intimate and she participates with her Haitian friends in the jungles, caves and rocky ocean caverns of South East Haiti.

Printed in Great Britain
by Amazon

78574371R00050